REASON AND ANTI-REASON
IN OUR TIME

REASON AND
ANTI-REASON
IN OUR TIME

BY

KARL JASPERS

TRANSLATED BY
STANLEY GODMAN

NEW HAVEN
YALE UNIVERSITY PRESS

Printed in Great Britain

CONTENTS

I

I

THE CHALLENGE OF
THE SCIENTIFIC METHOD

THERE is no common ground among contemporary
philosophers. Thomism forms an exception for
those who believe in it, and far removed from it
intellectually there are the schools and literary
movements centred round a single master, the most
successful of which are Marxism and psychoanalysis.
In these short lectures I do not propose to discuss
any one problem. That would presuppose the common ground we lack. I wish to draw attention to the
essential and general factor of philosophical thinking
in which we may be able to re-discover a common
ground. I mean the self-evident faculty of Reason,
which is as old as the hills, has sometimes been
buried or frivolously despised, has always to be
acquired anew and can never be entirely consummated.

Since the day in 1901 when I first entered the
University of Heidelberg and these very rooms as a

[7]

student I have always regarded Reason as the essence of philosophy. After the experience of fifty years in the university and the outside world my knowledge of its nature is still incomplete.

Science is an indispensable constituent of Reason. That is my theme today. Tomorrow I shall speak about Reason itself; the day after tomorrow on Reason in the conflicts of our time.

I propose to take Marxism and psychoanalysis as my texts and by criticising these familiar phenomena to point to science as the condition of all true philosophy.

Marx sees history as a single whole. From the original state of a non-violent, egalitarian but only semi-conscious and completely untechnical, society history moved on through the sins of the division of labour, private property and class distinctions to a tremendous development of knowledge and skill, especially in the bourgeois era which ushered in modern technics. According to Marx, the process will continue until it reaches the final state in which the egalitarian community will be restored in a non-violent and therefore stateless society, bringing with it a new and unprecedented advance in human skill and productivity. The historical evolution of labour is the key to an understanding of the whole of history. The laws of economics are not eternal but vary with each new form of society and its methods of production. They are historically determined; they rise and pass away.

The method by which this process is understood is dialectic, which is both a pattern of thought and a pattern of history. All the apparent fixed states of history and society are being repeatedly shaken by the transition into their antitheses until the perfect synthesis will be achieved in the harmonious freedom of all. Until that consummation every phase of history will create the forces by which it will be overcome. The movement of history produces the State as a function of power acting in the interests of the ruling class; it produces ideologies to justify the power of the state but it also produces the science and technics which will one day serve the classless society as an everlasting acquisition.

All this Marx attempted to prove and confirm with economic and sociological discoveries. But as he gathers his facts and his far-ranging material and works out his ingenious economic theories he is inspired by the fundamental conviction that history is ripe for the final revolution, that the ultimate transition which will bring about the truth, justice

[9]

and freedom of the classless society, is imminent.

All previous revolutions have meant merely the downfall of one group and the seizure of power by another, whilst the general situation, including the division and exploitation of labour, remained unchanged. The Communist revolution will transform the whole situation and bring about a corresponding change in man himself. Man will become completely different and capable only after this total change has taken place of founding the new society. At present the process of history still estranges man from himself through the division of labour, the false machine system (which will be overcome only by the perfect technical system of the future), through money, through the purely commercial attitude to things, and so on. In the proletarian, man has attained the condition of utter forsakenness. But only through this total loss will the dialectical transition into the opposite, that is, the complete recovery of man, become possible.

This first and final revolution, the real revolution which will embrace the whole being of man, is certainly coming but it will be brought about by man himself. The inevitability of the historical process coincides with man's freedom of action. All previous philosophies of history have been founded on passive contemplation; this one is active: it acts through its very thought. For, to act in conformity with historical necessity, a scientific basis is required. Marx provided it. And he shows what he intends to do with it when he writes the threatening words: 'Philosophers have so far merely interpreted the world in different ways; their real business should be to change it.'

For Marx, the passion for justice and the revolt against injustice which have been attempted so often and in vain, will be changed by this new philosophy since they will leave the timeless world of the Ought for the rough and tumble of real history. If man stands with both feet firmly set on the ground of history he can take historical action, as a step towards justice, with what has ripened in his age. But if he merely acts from a vacuum and is out of touch with actual history, he himself will be destroyed.

On principle, therefore, Marx rejected the absolute in favour of a historical standard of judgement. And this ever-changing standard is acquired, he believes, by knowledge of history as a whole. For this the scientific method is necessary.

Hitherto, to find perfect happiness, men have conceived Utopias of the just society, they have

[11]

planned idyllically peaceful communities. Marx's advance 'from Utopia to science' rules out all such futilities and works on the basis of knowledge of the real process of history.

From the slave revolts of antiquity to the Peasants' wars and even later, the masses have often attempted to improve their lot by organising rebellions. But because they were blind to the real facts of the situation they only succeeded in destroying themselves and making the condition of their class even worse. Now, however, effective political action is prepared on the basis of scientifically valid insights, in order to bring about by force the total revolution which is imminent in any case.

The influence of Marx is threefold: scientific, philosophical and political.

(a) As an important theoretical economist he has his place among others. His influence on sociological thought is great. To read his writings for the first time is an illumination even today. As a historian he made many intelligent observations and shed a penetrating light on contemporary events. In economic research he is an active force, both positively and negatively. The conclusions of his that have been absorbed into the mainstream of knowledge and the arguments that have been critically refuted cover a wide field. But all this would not have made him the towering and unique force that he represents in the modern world.

(b) Marx is a philosopher, even in his purely scientific work. He is never interested in details for their own sake. His insight is total. All his investigations into particular topics are intended to confirm and elaborate a fixed insight into the whole process of history. This total insight, however, is part of a philosophical faith which we may attempt to describe as follows. All previous philosophy has been ideological. Only in our own time has it had the chance to become true; first, because it has ceased merely to contemplate the world and is setting out to change it, and secondly, because it has now become nothing less than the one and only science. This twofold change has finished philosophy as understood hitherto. The new philosophy even discards the name; it calls itself 'materialism', which does not mean the materialism of physics and chemistry but the recognition of labour and production as the basic human reality and the thesis that they are the source of every other human reality. This new materialism acknowledges no transcendence whatsoever. The world is the whole reality. And the world is the material world of labour

[13]

and nothing else. With the creation of this world man creates himself. Man is the ultimate being, self-sufficient, the creator of himself and his world. Religion, on the other hand, conceals reality, paralyses human activity, is an instrument of oppression because it hides oppression and makes it bearable. Religion is the opium of the people.

This philosophical faith believes in the One; not in the one God, however, but in the one united science which includes the unity of science and action, science and philosophy. This 'unified' science may be roughly described thus: history is a part of natural history, of the evolution of nature into man. Natural science, therefore, in all its fields, already refers to man and is essentially a human science. But the science of man includes natural science as an ever-changing product of the human mind. Hence there will be only one science and that is the science of history.

The authentic all-embracing science is definitively attained by Marx. Objectivity and impartiality are untrue, in his view, because they destroy the unity of science and maintain an unhistorically absolute truth. He requires all to participate in this new faith which is based on scientific insights and is not, as in former times, merely ideological in character. To participate in it means to reject objectivity and to accept the dialectical truth of historical evolution at the point where it stands at present.

The reward of this new faith is that it allows the believer to have a good conscience despite his bias, since he can believe that the bias is itself historically true. In its method of communication this type of thought is inevitably a form of propaganda. The style is not that of impartial scholarship. Counter-arguments are not quoted; facts which tell against the thesis propounded are ignored; only those that endorse it are considered at all. The advocates of this faith believe with religious fervour that they are in possession of perfect truth. They do not have scientific certainty.

In contrast to the unifying science of Marxism, however, authentic modern science of every kind is essentially particular, leading to cogent, methodically sound, objective insights, recognising no universal method, adapting its methods to the nature of the object under scrutiny. The unifying 'science' of Marxism has nothing in common with modern science. The Marxist form of 'science' is rather a mode of total knowledge of the kind that has been accepted as valid in the great philosophical systems of the past. This merely would-be science has become quite untenable from the standpoint of the critical method of modern science. Marx's 'total knowledge' can be unmasked as a form of the would-be science that Hegel produced and Marx repeated, taking the old-fashioned form and filling it with a specifically modern content.

It is typical of every faith that it rejects unbelief. Believing that he was in possession of a total system of knowledge Marx, like the theologians, was the enemy of agnosticism and scepticism. He rejected Kant, for example, regarding him as a sceptic whose philosophy reflects 'the impotence, depressed condition and wretchedness of the German middle class'. The great force of Marxist thought obviously lies in its fundamentally false interpretation of faith as a science. The power of its fanatical certainty is derived from a belief which the term 'science' disguises. What is in fact a purely personal faith is dubbed 'scientific'. It never calls itself a faith though it behaves like any other dogmatic faith: it is blind to everything that runs counter to it; it is aggressive and incapable of communication.

(c) Marx the scientist and Marx the philosophical believer are inseparable from Marx the politician. In reality the political has priority. His political influence operates as the influence of a faith: his faith itself is political. Marx and the Marxists are warriors of faith. Since Marx has no illusions about the realities of force and power he gives them a decisive place in his programme of action. He always takes into account the practical effectiveness of every move he makes. He is against talk and discussion; he wants faithful followers. His first target is the dictatorship of the proletariat. It can only be achieved by violence. Marx exercises no conscious control over his will to power. The true faith justifies the means. This political creed imagines it can do what no previous political system has ever been able to do. As it has a 'total' understanding of history it can make and carry out 'total' plans.

If, agreeing with Marx, we see the three entities of science, faith and politics as a unity, we shall see the intellectual tragedy for which he was responsible when he destroyed science in the name of science. Perhaps this can best be explained by considering the meaning of dialectic. Dialectic is the motion produced by the turning of everything into its opposite. It is a motion that takes place in the mind and in things themselves. Marx makes this process absolute. According to him, everything is dialectic; he adds that what previously happened unconsciously

B   [17]

but in fact dialectically, will henceforth be done consciously and thus freedom and necessity will coincide.

The results that follow from this conception are astonishing. Dialectic becomes causality. The laws of dialectic are interpreted as laws of causality. Dialectic becomes the sole cause of all historical occurrences, explaining all events as radical transitions. It also expects by actively intensifying any particular historical process to transform it into its opposite, which means, to take a concrete example, that if I urge on to the utmost of my ability the destruction of the capitalist world, with its ideologies, ethics and so-called rights of man (in the Marxist view, all merely part and parcel of the bourgeois era), then I expect, by so doing, to hasten the transition to the age of the new and real 'total' man. Destruction is creative. If I bring about nothingness, new being will set in automatically. This is of course both theoretically and practically simply a conjuror's trick, dressed up as a pseudo-science.

The second result is the use of dialectic as a means of substantiating the desire of the moment. Dialectic becomes the most effective form of sophistry. There is no eternal Truth, no eternal Reason. All reality is history. History is movement. Movement is

[18]

dialectical transition. Whoever is involved in it will, from his superior knowledge, unhesitatingly change every position into its opposite. Anyone who wants to hold on to something instead of changing it, and attempts to substantiate his case with Marxist doctrine or even with facts, will be told that he is a bourgeois reactionary and must learn to think dialectically. The heads of the wretched faithful are set in a whirl and made capable of taking up any position or doing any action or obeying any command—for it is in fact obedience to the dialectic of history with which my wise teacher is more familiar than I. This new science ends by so completely bewildering the faithful that they are left in total confusion with no alternative but to follow its commands.

This fundamental confusion is so dangerous because it seems to be peculiar to our age and recurs in other movements. Owing to the scientific successes of recent centuries a superstitious belief has developed which expects everything from science and the technical devices for which it is responsible. Since there is no longer anything above man there is a tendency to put him in the place of God and to regard history and not the deity as the final court of appeal.

[19]

Marx became a prophet in a God-forsaken world in the forms appropriate to this world. He appeared as the herald of science, but of a science that is in fact not a science at all. He came as one who commands in the name of history, not in the name of God. The monstrous falseness of this alleged unity of faith, science and action, of the attempt to prove and justify everything by dialectic seems totally transparent, but the mere fact that such a faith exists is enough to fill one with horror and amazement, for only destruction and purposeless violence can spring from the attempt to give reality to an absurdity.

Psychoanalysis, now an active force throughout the world, makes extraordinary promises, it claims to provide absolute knowledge of man and to bring about perfect happiness. Having first developed in the field of medicine, it has invaded every department of human life and is now preparing to bring the whole of medicine into subjection to itself. It is beyond all dispute that the psychoanalytical movement has made a contribution to our knowledge of man, mainly through the discoveries of Freud. These discoveries have been incorporated in scientific psychiatry. Criticism of the psychoanalyst's methods of research, of the significance and limitations of the results obtained, has long since been carried out and I need not repeat it. Anyone interested in what is scientifically valid in psychoanalysis will assimilate it in the same way as he will assimilate the scientific truth in hypnotism, but he will be careful not to overrate its importance.

There are in the world today independent psychotherapists who love man and want to help him. They work as individuals using their own personal methods. They also use psychoanalytical methods but without becoming their slaves. They do not organise and make a matter of mechanical technique what must always remain a matter of personal communication between individuals. They will permit the so-called training analysis for those who ask for it of their own free will but will not demand it for scientific or dogmatic reasons and they will refuse to admit it as the condition which a psychoanalytical doctor must fulfil before he can be registered.

But in one of the trends developing within the psychoanalytical movement, which appears to be steadily increasing, something quite different is happening. Just as Marxism owes its influence not to the particular insights it has contributed to scientific knowledge but to its totalitarian approach and unscientific character, so it is with this type of psychoanalysis. Psychoanalysis as a faith is made possible by basic scientific errors, a few of which I shall briefly describe.[1] First, to understand the meaning of something is not to explain its cause. The understanding of the meaning of something takes place in mutual communication: causality is foreign to this process and means recognising something as different and distant. Understanding does not have an effect on things, but leaves the road open to freedom. Causal explanation enables one to intervene to some extent in the process of events, to steer it towards certain desired ends. But if I confuse the possibility of the understanding of meaning, in the realm of freedom, and causal explanation I am violating freedom; for then, I am treating it as an object, as if it were a perceptible object, which is to degrade it. In addition I shall miss causal possibilities which really exist.

Secondly, the character of therapeutical effects is questionable. It is known that all kinds of psycho-therapeutical processes have been successful in the hands of effective personalities throughout the ages. But psychoanalytical treatment has had as many successes and failures as other methods. The satis-

[1] See p. 92.

faction which some patients derive from a detailed analysis of themselves and of their whole life-history can scarcely be called a cure. Whereas in medicine proper, enormous almost incredibly successful cures have been made possible by the discoveries of the last hundred and fifty years, so that the average life of Western man has been extended by twenty years, it appears that the successes of psychotherapy have not increased at all. They can hardly do so owing to the very nature of things.

Thirdly, what is called neurosis is not characterised by the intelligible contents of phenomena but by the mechanism of transmuting spiritual into physical processes, by turning sensible into senseless physical occurrences. Only a tiny percentage of human beings suffers from this mechanism, this gift or fate, by which they encounter their own spiritual and intellectual processes, the acts of their own freewill transposed into physical phenomena, as something foreign to themselves and beyond their control. Most people repress, forget, leave unsettled, suffer and endure the worst without transforming it into physical symptoms.

These aberrations lie within the sphere of medical science. But the psychoanalysts, by arousing false hopes, lead those who become enslaved to them far

[23]

beyond the spheres of medicine and the sciences. They make possible something quite different.

First, the claim to have a total knowledge of man, of what he is before the division into body and soul. This 'total' conception of man, which is structurally analagous to totalitarianism in politics, is based on the confusion of the possibility of understanding with freedom. Freedom turned into an object is no longer freedom at all. The possibility of understanding brought into the flux of endless interpretation and re-interpretation is no longer a possibility of understanding.

Total knowledge is correlated with practice. Psychoanalysis and being psychoanalysed becomes the real life and the deepest satisfaction of those who believe in it. It is the materialisation of a belief in the flux of endless symbolic metamorphoses and descents into hell. This belief, though apparently in a constant movement of criticism, resists all criticism of its principles. It refuses to listen. But it is able to indulge in the infinite material of possible meanings and symbolic fixations. The development of the movement into an orthodox faith which began with Freud's sentence of excommunication on unfaithful disciples, is a trend inherent in the nature of the method. By way of societies claiming the power to impose their faith on others this trend could lead to the formation of sects, with incalculable results in the shape of hostility to and estrangement from science, inhumanity and irrationalism. The unconditional requirement of the so-called training analysis is the first step in this direction.

We may well ask what are the conditions and origins of such a 'faith'.

Externally, it is part and parcel of the capitalistic world in which people can afford this kind of luxury. In addition, it attracts the semi-educated. Both the primitive man, unspoilt by education, and the well-educated man of high intelligence, are apparently impervious to these methods. The extraordinary successes they have achieved in literature, the popularity they enjoy and the appreciation they have received even from outsiders have produced a feeling of jubilation and a confidence in ultimate victory in the psychoanalysts, though, like the Marxists, they are always moaning about injury and persecution and some of them tend indignantly to repudiate all human interests outside their sphere. In view of their successes one does wonder what lies behind such a great and persistent fashion. Presumably it responds to a genuine need; though obviously in a way that is anything but genuine.

It is evident that there is a perverted section of humanity in the world today that longs for 'liberation'. Psychoanalysis gives it an illusory liberation which is as untrue as the humanity of which it is the reflection. The demand to escape from a state of perversion is genuine. But a valid answer to this need, such as would be provided by a world order in which, if man were accepted, he would become sure of himself, does not exist in this age. Order is replaced by every kind of violence, fanaticism and terrorism. The great problem that faces our present age is how to create a reality in which human existence can find fulfilment and rise into what is infinitely open. So long as the process of disintegration continues, any valid answer can come only from individuals speaking with individuals from the depths of our historical foundations. To state this truth is, however, much more difficult than to see through the error. The psychoanalyst, so far as I can see, only appears to provide solutions.

Psychoanalysis becomes an attitude to life which —in keeping with the requirements of the age— understands itself scientifically, not as a cult or as magic, but is in fact deprived of real science and is a new form of magic. It is an attitude marked by universal scepticism and, at the same time, by a readiness to accept any possible interpretation. For example, if something cannot be explained by a repression, a 'total' biography of the patient is employed. If this explanation also fails, something like the Indian doctrine of karma, of a pre-temporal act of freedom, of guilt from an earlier life, is tried, as when cancer is interpreted as the result of a free cause in man himself. In this way psychoanalysis becomes the ruin of the scientific method.

What we are witnessing is an enormous process of self-deception conditioned by the age we live in, which bewitches its victims, who find in it the satisfaction of their lives. But the source of the process is so false that it is bound to confuse hopelessly not only the knowledge of those who are swept into it but their whole being.

Our scientific attitude becomes reliable only as we reflect on its methodological presuppositions. Such reflection leads to a separation of the various methods of scientific enquiry from the methods of philosophical thought. This separation provides a wide and essential field for study and reflection. I want to point to one basic idea only, a simple one which, once it is grasped, brings about a change in the meaning of all our knowledge. This is the idea: all knowledge in the world refers to particular objects and is acquired with definite methods from definite points of view. Therefore it is wrong to make any knowledge absolute. This mistake is made, however, because of a very understandable illusion: we identify the objective being of any particular thing with absolute being, objects with Being itself. We must work our way out of this deception, which takes place precisely when an object is perceived with the utmost definition, when the understanding of a particular orientation is regarded as knowledge of being itself. We must liberate ourselves from enslavement to objects by taking a basic philosophical operation which will enable us to soar into the 'Comprehensive'.

This is easily said and difficult to accomplish. As a principle it is simple to grasp but perhaps never wholly achieved. For the whole clarity of the 'Comprehensive' is only transmitted to us through the clearly-defined objectiveness which we find within the subject-object dichotomy. The Comprehensive can only be grasped indirectly within the schism in which for our conscious understanding all Being must appear as objectivity. With our whole nature we seek for Being itself, but in scientific

[28]

knowledge we find it only in objects which hide it because of their tendency to become absolute.

Once we have understood that, the structure of the meaning of knowledge, not of factual knowledge, is changed in the sciences themselves. The meaning of knowledge appears no longer as the possibility of a single comprehensive theory of Being, not as a dogmatic picture of total knowledge, which is incomplete but exists in principle and only needs elaborating—but merely as a methodological system which shows me by what processes and what means I encounter particular objects. Such methodologically conscious knowledge saves us from transmuting particular knowledge into a dogmatic absolute; it liberates us from any specific theory by making us aware of the meaning of theory itself.

In particular, a consciousness of method can preserve us from a perversion which forces itself on us against our will and attempts to subjugate us again and again. Our scientific knowledge can only go as far as reality is grasped by our methods and enclosed within our categories. The presuppositions of the experiential sciences do not provide a knowledge of experience as a whole. It is true that, given these presuppositions, and those which will come to light, I can know *ad infinitum*, but I cannot anticipate

[29]

the infinite and make it an object of which I imagine I have already perceived the fundamentals.

It is only when using the methodologically clarified sciences that I know what I know and what I do not know. By applying specific criteria to specific knowledge I can acquire binding knowledge of things in the world. The difference is between knowing in a closed building and being open to all the perspectives of the infinite world. When I grasped that in my younger days, I tried to put the scientific method into practice in my 'Psycho-pathology', not by presenting the whole field of psychiatric understanding dogmatically but by throwing light on its methods. As regards its contents this book is a scientific work; with respect to the deliberately chosen form in which it is written it is a work of philosophy.

*

But now comes the crucial point: once we have grasped the meaning of scientific method—it has come into universal view only in the last few centuries (and is perhaps the greatest event in the history of the world since the creative climacteric around 500 B.C.)—we see science as the condition of all truth in philosophy itself. Without science truthfulness in philosophical thinking is no longer possible today.

We profess an unconditional belief in modern science as the way to truth.

The radical undermining of the modern mind—which has been expounded and discussed so often—is not an undermining of modern science. In so far as its methods are above-board, modern science has not been shaken at all, but has become progressively more trustworthy, lucid and assured—within its limits.

What has been shattered for many people is the meaning of science; they no longer take the necessity of science for granted. To regain this meaning requires other sources than science itself can provide.

It is not easy to understand science. One must have participated in it to have a trustworthy idea of what it is. If one has no inside knowledge of science and thinks of it merely in terms of its externals, of the wrong tracks it has sometimes taken, of its transposition of means into ends, of its technical applications, then one will misinterpret it, as did Scheler and Count Keyserling, as an expression of the will to power. One will see it as guided merely by technics, brought into being by the will to power of modern technicians, and even as a perversion of the meaning of truth, of historically disastrous significance.

This misinterpretation of science is equivalent to an assault on the Reason which science needs. The evil consequences of subjecting science to the will to power have already shown themselves. They have to be countered with reason and science itself. The source of science is not the will to power over things (though such power has in fact occasionally had a stimulating effect on science) but the will to truth. The most admirable, selfless and unassuming men, inspired by the human capacity for knowledge, have their place among the great scientists and scholars of the last few centuries (not excluding such figures as Bacon and Descartes who may nevertheless have contributed something to the misinterpretation of science as a product of the will to power). The will to truth, this source of human dignity, is the origin of modern science and its character; it is the sovereignty of man's freedom to know.

Derogatory assertions about science are caused only by blindness to its true meaning; but they spring to some extent from a mood of total historical despair, from an eschatological attitude which cannot be proved and cannot be refuted, except philosophically by a discussion of Reason itself. For decades now, these derogatory assertions have been finding a response and preparing men to promote by their own behaviour the disasters they see in progress all around them. Those who have succumbed usually keep aloof from practical affairs or throw themselves headlong into them with fanatical blindness, helping to bring about the catastrophe they believe in.

The misunderstanding of science would hardly be possible, however, if science were self-sufficient. But even the choice of subjects for scientific research cannot be derived from science itself. The meaning and necessity of science cannot be verified by its own structure. Science is not self-supporting. Where it tries to be, it falls into an infinite abyss of platitudes. Scientific research always encounters an initial act which is the presupposition but not part of science itself.

Dissatisfaction with science is the expression of the will to truth which reaches out beyond the fulfilment that science can provide. Marxism, psychoanalysis and all the many other pseudo-sciences would not be so effective if they did not appeal to a desire for truth different from that which science satisfies, a desire that demands to be fulfilled. On what frontier of science do these pseudo-sciences offer their services? On the frontier of this fact that science,

c   [33]

where it is pure, does not reveal Being itself nor the whole of truth but only objects in the world, though in an infinite progress. Fundamentally we want more than science can give.

What we have to decide is—are we going to seek this 'more than science can give' in experience, in the occult and the irrational, or in the attempt to prove the origin of our possible existence in Reason? If we take the second way the mind will be set free to illuminate what is not scientifically knowable— here too by making conscious and methodological use of philosophical methods. Then the language of all things will become audible, myths full of meaning, poetry and art the 'organ of philosophy' (Schelling). But we shall not confuse the language of myth with concrete knowledge. That which is perceived in contemplation and inspires action must neither be extinguished nor acquire the character of knowledge, if its truth is forced to pass the test of Reason. This truth cannot be tested by experience but by our own Being, the rise or fall of our authentic existence and the contents of our love.

But even this perception illuminated by thought always occurs within the dichotomy of subject and object. Only by confronting an object can we obtain a clear idea of what lies before and beyond the dichotomy. Everything of which we are to obtain a clear, immediate notion must enter into the subject-object dichotomy. This dichotomy cannot be talked out of existence; it can only be understood. Only in and through the illumination which it provides can we truly and really overcome it.

Philosophy makes it clear that subject and object belong to each other; the one cannot exist without the other. But inside this ever present relationship there is an essential difference between subject and object—taking the subject to mean existence, consciousness, the possibility of existence—and hence an essential difference in the way subject and object are related to each other. It will help us to see the difference if we ask: with what subject are we relating ourselves to which object?—how is the variety in the subject-object relationship constituted, what is its structure?—with what subject do we attain the evidence of a truth?—where do we confuse the natures of subject and object?—where and of what kind is the way to the unity of all the modes of subjective and objective being?

Let me sum up. The substitutes for faith, of which we selected Marxism and psychoanalysis, and their rejection of authentic modern science in the name of a 'science' of their own devising are not, in our view, simply an error. They are the result of a basic trend in the modern world: the urge to be freed from freedom. There is a desire to forget the possibility of authentic personal being and to rely on a world of history which men think they can understand, or on a reality understood in terms of psychology which is considered to be what one is and can be. In short, one relies on a false, total 'knowledge'. There is a desire to relegate to a totality of knowledge what only the individual can do, that from which the state and society and the reality of man receive their ground, direction and absolute meaning. There is a desire to achieve by 'total planning' a state of affairs which will produce happiness automatically. What is intended is a well-organised society of animals rather than a community of those who recognise a constant claim upon them and persevere in the way of freedom.

But we must not in any sense look upon the current of affairs as inevitable and immutable, as something that nobody can alter. Consciousness of the actual powerlessness of the individual at any particular moment of history has led to a 'total' view objectivised into an absolute pseudo-knowledge. The metaphysical or gnostic 'total' knowledge of an event of Being is no more than an evil or beautiful dream.

Though we cannot see the total process we can see how 'total' knowledge and 'total' planning, which proceeds from it, are leading to growing chaos, to the destruction of organic societies and their replacement by mechanised orders controlled by terror. We can see how psychoanalysis tends to change man into the likeness of the image which it produces of him and how, as a result of this change, man's spirit falls into a state of demoralisation which he calls disease and which the supposedly healing methods of psychoanalysis only make worse.

What is it that is being sacrificed and abandoned on all these wrong tracks? It cannot be demonstrated or observed and it is not something that can be shown objectively. It cannot be represented in anything visible, myth or poem. It is that which man can be when he becomes himself. It is the possibility of human existence, and it is this by means of Reason.

The errors we have been describing can be overcome by taking two steps; first by acquiring the scientific method which enables us to see through the untruth of 'total' knowledge and pseudo-mythical objectivisations, and which, positively, provides the foundation of all truthfulness; and secondly by taking a leap into the imageless, unobjectifiable, self-impelling source of our self, which is Reason.

[37]

II

REASON

IN THE first lecture I spoke of the scientific method as the presupposition of all true thinking. To understand science, to acquire the scientific attitude as a reliable approach to truth, demands the kind of experimentation that every student begins for himself in laboratories, seminars, institutes and on his own, i.e. by methodical intercourse with things themselves—and this requires a methodological consciousness. But science is not adequate to embrace Truth. We are now to speak of that 'more than science', of Reason which is the meaning of science and which leads to the demand for science.

In common parlance Reason is identical with intellect. It can in fact take no step without the intellect, but it goes beyond it. What is Reason? This great theme of philosophy has not been exhausted by the thinking of the millennia and can never be exhausted by systematic thought. Let me try to characterise Reason.

Reason has no assured stability: it is constantly on the move. Once it has gained a position it presses on to criticise it and is therefore opposed to the tendency to free oneself from the necessity for all further thought by once and for all accepting irrevocably fixed ideas. It demands a careful thoughtfulness—it is therefore the opposite of mere capriciousness. It leads to self-knowledge and knowledge of limits, and therefore to humility—and it is opposed to intellectual arrogance. It demands a constant listening and it is able to wait—it is therefore opposed to the narrowing furies of passion.

Thus Reason works itself out of the chains of dogma, of caprice, of arrogance, of passion. But where does it lead to? Reason is the will to unity. The impulse of reason and the prospect of its increasing brightness spring from the question: what is this unity?

Reason refuses to take hold of any kind of unity but seeks the real and only unity. It knows that it is lost if it clutches prematurely at a part of truth and makes it the ultimate and absolute truth. It wills the One, which is All. It must not leave out anything, must not drop anything, exclude anything. It is in itself a boundless openness.

Even if it derives the criterion of the universally

valid from its own nature, it does not seem to acknowledge this criterion as absolutely valid. For in order not to lose the unity of the universal it immediately tackles what is left unexplained by this criterion, that is, the intrusive exceptions and the incomprehensible demands of historical authority. But it does not stop even there, for these too are, measured by the challenge of the ultimate unity, merely a provisional stage in the process of time. Reason can find no rest in the glory and splendour of the world nor can it ever stop asking questions.

Reason is attracted by what is most alien to it. It wants to illuminate and give being and language even to the passions of the night which threaten to destroy the laws that govern the day. It does not allow them to disappear into nothingness. Reason strives to avoid the sin of forgetfulness and self-deception, losing the One in a harmony that is only apparent. It presses on constantly to the place where unity is broken through in order that in this break-through it may grasp the truth that is in it. By breaking up every attractive semblance of unity (whose insufficiency is thereby proved) it attempts to ward off the metaphysical breach and rending of Being itself, the real Unity. Reason, itself the origin of order, attends even the powers which

[40]

destroy order. It is always there listening to that which is most alien to it, to that which breaks in upon it, to that which fails it.

Reason wants to draw near to everything that is and that must therefore be able to find expression in speech, in order to preserve it and give it a validity of its own.

In order to be able to seek the One, the seeker himself must become one. This is the demand that recurs unforgettably, but none too often, in the history of philosophy. Plato considered that man was himself only when he had become one with himself, only when he did not contradict himself. He saw it as man's greatest calamity to be at variance with himself, always changing his opinions and personality, inconsistent, whirled around by chance. Kant repeated this and Weininger is probably right in saying that 'Kant's ethic is the only one which does not try to blur the hard stern inner voice of the One with the noise of the Many'. He recalls Goethe's saying: 'One can lose everything, so long as one remains what one is' and Ibsen's Brand: 'And your sacrifices?—all idols, substitutes for the eternal God. . . . The victor's prize?—the unity of the will.'

Aiming at the unity of the One, Reason wants to

[41]

help everything that is to obtain its rights. But Reason, which is able to awaken all the sleeping origins, does not produce anything from itself. Penetrating into the heart of all that is, it can make the heart beat and show itself, but in order to become effective it must not miss the heart of all things.

Reason therefore points to both that unattainable One, whose infinite attraction makes Reason think, and to the origins, which, brought to life by Reason, attain the power of speech. Reason brings it about that what is and can be must unfold itself; it is that which unlocks the heart of everything. And it urges on into relation with the One that which it has unlocked, that it may not sink into the nothingness of diffusion.

I should now like to complete this short description of Reason by mentioning some of the possibilities brought about by Reason.

Reason is one with the boundless will to communication. Reason, because it is intent on and open to the One in all that is, refuses to break off communication. If the break in the sphere of existence is brought about by force, it can never recognise this as fundamentally necessary. With imperturbable confidence in the boundless possibilities of the whole of Being, Reason demands that the risk of communication should be taken again and again. To deny communication is tantamount to denying Reason itself.

But more, for Reason, in temporal existence, truth is bound up with communication. Truth that cannot be communicated becomes identical with untruth. Truth that binds itself to communication is not complete; it listens for an echo as it communicates itself, testing itself and the other. It is distinct from all one-sided proclamation. It is not I who bring the truth by myself: I can only seek for truth, along with the other who meets me, by listening, asking and testing.

Truth cannot be consummated in time because communication is not consummated. The incompleteness of communication manifests a depth which can be filled by nothing except Transcendence or Being which does not become, but simply *is*, beyond being and becoming.

Now we can say that, if God is eternal, then for man in time truth is the truth that develops in communication.

But the incompleteness of communication and thereby of truth disappears in the presence of Transcendence. The continuous horizontal line of time in which we live is intersected by the vertical line of the unknown One which bestows meaning and fulfilment on the truth we receive in communication. This basic reality is recalled in symbols, in images of a pre-temporal origin of the temporal necessity for communication or of an ultimate perfection of eternal harmony in which communication is surmounted. In the beginning was the One, the Truth to which we now have no access. But the One that we have lost calls from the depths of all temporality as if all the scattered fragments of truth should, through communication, be recovered from their present dispersal into the peace of the primal unity; though the forgotten Truth can never again be attained in time, it is constantly present in the movement that presses on towards it.

Reason is the realm in which this boundless communication takes place. But it is only a minimum. For the power of communication originates in love, in historical existence not unhistorical Reason, which itself receives its impulse and fulfilment from love. But this minimum lends momentum to philosophy. It makes possible the high moments of free Reason between men who are still very much strangers to one another, yet with Reason's help meet one another in the realm of absolute possibility.

[44]

In such encounters Reason is not yet the reality of love but it is freedom and therefore the condition of the truth and purity of love.

A further possibility of Reason is radical disengagement as a way of approach to the origin of the One.

We are tempted to raise to the status of the One what has developed into finality in innumerable historical facts. But Reason takes hold of the negative faculties of the intellect, which show the limits of everything, which are able to undermine critically every finality and are even capable of disregarding everything that is. Leibniz, Kant and Schelling all raised the question which Schelling stated thus: Why does anything at all exist; why does not nothing exist?—a question that is obviously very easy to ask and may seem to arise from an empty toying with ideas, one to which an intelligent answer is impossible. Nevertheless, it engaged the attention of the philosophers we have mentioned. It gave them the experience of losing all their foundations. It suggested that only a completely new mode of all knowledge of Being could enable them to regain new foundations. The question makes us conscious of the presence of Being as the unintelligible and impenetrable mystery that approaches us and exists before all our thought. The simple question, meaningless to the intellect, is for Reason a form which makes it possible for our existence, by taking this idea as its guide, to soar out of all finite constraints to the place whence we come, to the place which is before all worlds.

This all-embracing Reason, ignoring all finite certainties and relating itself directly to the One, suddenly brings everything that is to existence in a new, miraculously transparent way, making it speak as never before.

Reason effects yet another mode of disengagement. The Eternal becomes the present only in historical forms. Historicity is existentially the unity of time and eternity: what is eternal becomes definite as a phenomenon in time. We are historical existences, not examples of a generalisation. This historicity implies both fullness and being bound. We are identical with it. But we transcend it by becoming conscious of its nature through Reason. We are able, whilst still preserving our historicity, to return home to the supra-historical.

Imprisoned in historicity, without Reason, we become restricted to the narrow limits of existence, because we fail to perceive its historicity. But by lifting us out of our imprisonment Reason brings us to the first full awareness of our historicity and prepares a place for us where we are not at home but in relation to which we feel more at home.

Reason would certainly like to be able to grasp intellectually what this is which is before all phenomena, before all time, before all worlds, and which is equally after all phenomena, all time and all worlds—yet which is really neither before nor after, but something *in* phenomena, in time, in the world, namely, real, unhistorical Being itself. It is that which does not become, it is that which is. But Reason cannot think it; it can only keep it undefiled by the false thinking that would strive to enclose it in categories, images and verbal structures.

While we are speaking of Reason much might be said of its ramifications, of its concrete accomplishments. But we must inevitably describe all this and its foundations and what it is as a whole in historical modes of expression. When we imagine that we sometimes know more than we can think and express in historical forms, we are forced to look round for metaphors.

In another language Buddhists and Taoists speak of the Nothing, of the Emptiness to reach which is fullness itself. The Empty is conceived as the Receptive, as the all-embracing that is less than each

[47]

Being and is more than all—the Nothing that
contains the wealth of the All as a possibility and
which is a reality in the wise man who has acquired
knowledge. Once it has been affirmed, this Nothingness wavers inevitably in the ambiguity between
the Being that is a guide for those who have attained
it and the absolute Emptiness which is the unfillable
abyss. We can come to understand many formulae
of this all-embracing thought, in which everything
is first disregarded and then restored, by analogy to
Reason.

If the Emptiness of the Asiatics and the Reason
of the West seem to coincide anywhere, then it is
in the origin on which both strike, not in some
abstractly conceivable common element. But the
historical appearance of this comprehensive Truth,
in form and gesture, semblance and environment,
this absolutely non-general, this mystery of appearance is not the mere individuality of all natural
phenomena but this individuality raised to the level
of and eliminated by the spirit, inspired by existence,
sublimated and permeated by the Transcendence
which, through it, appears to speak in time as
Reason in an absolutely historical form.

If, in an attempt to make a radical distinction
between East and West, we oppose the movement

[48]

of the Westerner to the tranquillity of the Asiatic, all we find is a polarity in Reason itself which is the property of both East and West. This is the tension which is historically visible both here and there but whose appearance cannot be adequately expressed in abstract terms. Historicity itself never becomes a knowable object. We know nothing essential of one another except when we enter into communication.

Phenomena occurring when Reason is absent are innumerable. One principle of Unreason is the will to existence which claims precedence for itself. To make the contrast clear we may say: Reason connects, mere existence separates. The will to existence only wills itself, sees everything else as a means of strengthening its own existence. Existence conceals its self-will in the garb of objectivity, hides its loneliness in phrases about community and gestures of affection.

Reason, on the other hand, keeps the way open to the Comprehensive, deepens every bond by illuminating it, secures the continuity of existence. Unreason shuts up existence in itself, denies what has been said and done. Pride and selfishness enjoin forgetfulness if it is profitable to forget; they destroy loyalty towards others and towards oneself. By becoming absorbed in one's own existence, separation from the outside world becomes absolute, the emptiness of isolation. Such lives are without support from the past and have to start from the beginning over and over again. Thus everything appears to vanish into nothingness.

Whilst thought in the service of Reason is critical and seeks Truth, mere existence seeks to justify itself in sophistry and to bolster its self-assurance with the superstition of metaphysical gnosis.

And now comes the decisive point: Reason does not exist by nature but only by decision. It does not happen automatically like a natural event and like the whole of human life, in so far as it is natural, but arises from freedom. The decision becomes conscious in view of the human community when every single individual finds his self by the act of knowing what he wants.

Let us first look at human society. There is an optimistic belief that Truth will succeed in the end. We must confess that we do not trust this belief. Truth can be destroyed. The history of heresy is, to a large extent, the history of the violent destruction of truth in its historical reality. Totalitarian states show that whole populations can be reduced to ignorance by the withholding of news, the prohibition of free public discussion, and by becoming accustomed to constantly repeated falsehoods.

Optimism declares further that Truth always produces good results. But Truth can have such terrible results for our finite point of view that Schiller wrote: 'Only error makes life bearable and truth would be death.'

Only when we have realised what an ambiguous and indeed inexhaustible depth of meaning is connected with the word 'Truth' in such statements, only when we have convinced ourselves that truth is really Truth only in connexion, and in the totality of all connexions and stages, and is therefore still bound up in some way or another with un-truth in the setting of time and finiteness, and that this can only be explained by detailed philosophical enquiry—only then can we acquire, in place of a rash optimism, a confidence in truth which, although it cannot be proved, already has the character of a decision and a faith.

This is the comprehensive truth that Goethe had in mind when he said: 'Nothing is great but the truth and the smallest truth is great . . . even a harmful truth is useful, since it can only be momentarily

[51]

harmful and then leads to other truths which are always bound to become useful; conversely, a useful error is harmful, because it can only be momentarily useful and leads to other errors which are bound to become more and more harmful.'

This confidence in truth implies an unremitting striving after truth. The alleged truth which I believe I have when, in a rage, I cry 'I tell you, this is the truth!' is not truth. Truth lies rather in a process of continuous questioning and critical appropriation. To follow this path is identical with the decision to live in the world of un-reason and anti-reason in the strength of Reason, without knowing what will be the outcome; it means an incessant searching, trying and risking, all in a state of ignorance. It is a decision that can find no support for itself except through the self-illumination of the Reason which it achieves as it sees the phenomena and consequences of un-reason and anti-reason.

Let us look at the individual. Man does not find himself as a being endowed with reason; by a free act he turns, as it were, from the life that is given to him and takes the way of Reason. That he is able to do this is a mystery. He owes himself to himself and yet does not know how this is possible. He sees the limitation of his freedom, as he cannot use his will until he is free; but he cannot will freedom itself. Thus he knows that he is as it were a gift to himself, without knowing, learning or being made conscious by any reliable experience that he owes himself to another power. He knows that he is a gift to himself without knowing the giver; this state of being a gift to oneself, of owing oneself to oneself, requires all possible exertion, openness and good will.

The decision for Reason—which is also a decision for freedom, truth and the unconditionality of existential decision—is against nature, occurrence and necessity. One can call it the Unnatural as opposed to the 'innocence of nature'. It is the decision to acknowledge, first, one's guilt in choosing what is to be taken over, and second, one's responsibility in present decision. It means the rejection of the soporific and evil words of consolation: 'One must forget that such is life—what has happened was necessary, it could not be different.' On the contrary, I become free only in so far as I am conscious of my own guilt; otherwise I remain enslaved to nature. I become free only by an act of decision which is like a rebirth, a transformation, a revolution in my whole way of thinking. This is how Plato, the Bible and Kant saw it. Instead of taking things for granted, one begins to think for oneself, and this is the beginning of serious responsibility. One turns from a haphazard coming and going to the true origin of one's self—from complications that hide the essentials to the great simplicities, from aimless drifting to the decisive facts.

All our purposeful activities have a fulcrum in the world. Here in the revolution of philosophical decision something happens that has technically no fulcrum. It is the mystery and presence of the inner action, the intercourse with oneself, taking hold of the absolute. Here in this revolution is the source of all genuine, unconditional communication, the basis of reliability in the sphere of the incalculable.

Reason becomes existentially real only by a leap from the apparently closed reality of existence into the reality of Being itself. This revolution in the way of thinking, which is not open to psychological explanation, has been discussed by philosophers. There are hidden passages in their works which are obviously based on personal experience. I will take Kant as an example. He speaks of the character that is not a particular character, one among a number of possibilities, but the character a man gives himself by committing himself to immutable principles which he has set up for himself by the use of Reason. Of this character he says:

[54]

'The man who is aware of a special character in his way of thinking, does not have it by nature but must always have acquired it. One may also assume that a certain solemnity in the vows he takes makes the founding of this character and the time when this revolution takes place as memorable as a re-birth into a new epoch:—education and the examples of others cannot bring about this steadfastness in a man's principles step by step but only by a kind of explosion. Perhaps there are only a few who have attempted this revolution before their thirtieth year, and still fewer who have accomplished it before their fortieth.—It is futile to try to become a better man in parts . . . the founding of a character implies the absolute unity of a man's principles and his way of life. . . .' And then: 'In a word: truthfulness . . . established as the supreme maxim, is the only proof that a man has become conscious of having a character; and as to have this is the minimum that one may require of a man of Reason, but at the same time is also the maximum of the inner value (of human dignity): so it must be possible for someone endowed with common human Reason to be a man of principle.'

In the present, Koestler has described in remark-able and moving words the transformation which liberated him from Communism and made him the glowing advocate of freedom and humanity. He speaks of the 'experience' which 'as soon as one clothes it in words always appears in the false garb of the eternal commonplaces',—'that man is a reality and humanity an abstraction;—that one cannot treat men as figures in a political equation, because they behave like the signs for nil and infinity by which all mathematical calculations are upset;—that the end justifies the means only within very narrow limits;—that ethics is not merely a function of social utility and charity not a petty bourgeois sentiment but the force of gravitation which holds every civilisation together'. 'Nothing can sound duller', he writes, 'than when one tries to put into words an experience that by its very nature is impervious to language; and yet every single one of these trivial commonplaces was incompatible with the Communist faith.'

Koestler calls an 'experience' what was in fact a decision to change his whole way of thinking. As a man of letters and a publicist is he afraid of familiar words and phrases? Is this contempt for simple and familiar everyday language perhaps connected with the modern stress on originality and the devaluation of everything traditional? Is this why he falls back on such a well-worn and misleading term as 'experience'?

Is it true that the eternal commonplaces sound dull? This disparagement is understandable because these simple truths have so often been misused for shallow edification and mere chatter and loveless application. I want to refute such disregard for them. May it not be true that these simple statements are inexhaustible? Must they not be interpreted and assimilated ever anew, because their truth is unfathomable? Do not these old formulae still enshrine the basically essential truths for us even today?

Such principles as the Kantian maxim that man must never be made a mere means but should always remain an end in himself—or Plato's statement that ignorance is the greatest evil—or the Ten Commandments and the great eternal ideas of philosophy: all these are easily repeated but it needs more than mere intelligence, it needs Reason really to understand and assimilate them. Even today to make them one's own is the precondition of all philosophy that intends to be true.

The simple principles of philosophical Reason may appear meaningless formalities since as generalisations they are meaningless. But that is the very reason why they are of such comprehensive significance. They act like incantations which are nevertheless transparent to Reason. They recall what is decisive without imposing it on us. They open the eyes and stimulate the mind. Through their formality they are able, as it were, to open the eyes of our blindness but they leave the vision of the concrete to our freedom. They are not pronouncements, but they appeal to the Reason of those who come to meet them. Whoever hears them and makes them his own becomes different; he wins resolution.

Reason creates the mental space where everything that is can be caught, acquire language and hence validity as a being in its own right. This 'space' which Reason provides is like the water, air and light in which all life can thrive and it is therefore eager to be filled with such life, but on condition that it is permeated by Reason.

To put the same thing in another way: Reason illuminates the Absolute but does not itself provide the substance. It provides only the forms which need to be filled, in order to become temporal realities. It understands historicity but is itself essentially not historical. It provides the space for unconditionality in the substances of existence.

The frontier of Reason lies on the one side in the reality of life which it encounters as something alien to Reason, and on the other side, in that reality of existence which it can illuminate infinitely. Reason itself is borne by this existence, whilst existence only attains the fullness of reality through Reason. Reason and existence are inseparable.

Let us call to mind the unity of the movement of Reason and existence, in success and failure, by saying something about the love which is not Reason but is reasonable, so that Plato was able to conceive Eros and Knowledge as one.

Love is implanted in life, is unconditionally identified with it: it is historical. When love takes hold of me, it is as though I am real for the first time. I come to myself, everything that exists appears in a new light. Life becomes serious for the first time. Whatever I do now, it is as if it had been accepted or rejected by Eternity, as if it were either a memory of the eternal or a sinking into the abyss of nothingness.

When love is granted fulfilment, it is the happiness of unfolding life. Men, as it were, know one another again in time. The world becomes for them the language of Transcendence. Beyond the legal and the contractual and beyond the moral, men confide in the reliable though incalculable ground of the Transcendent. Life is played as a game on a ground of deepest seriousness, open to the Transcendent, growing in depth of presence under the shadow of the end that is coming to all life.

But love may fail to find fulfilment. One of the lovers may be lost through death, insanity or infidelity. The lover who is left forsaken seems to fade away. But from this fading there springs a strange life as if the lover himself had died and were now active somewhere else, patiently, as a devoted friend of man, but from an infinite distance, pining away unhappily because not able to be present in real life and yet so profoundly present as a different person that many now feel inexplicably attracted by him and transformed, and see him as a good demon in captivity who now belongs to no one, lavishing his care on casual encounters but not spending a vestige of himself. What really happens in such cases seems incapable of being objectified, is impossible to demonstrate as a fact; it cannot be stated conceptually; it can only be seen in silence, moving the heart and never to be forgotten.

Let us look at another kind of love: love for one's origins, for one's native country and historical roots, the love that knows it comes from one root. I know that even in the tiniest details of my daily environment I am supported and surrounded by my origins; I know that my life is guided by these foundations, and the more I become myself, the more decisively I take possession of them.

But this love can be upset. Man can be torn from his roots. The millions of emigrants, refugees and 'displaced persons'—above all in Europe and China—are learning this terrible reality for themselves. Love has lost the physical presence of the beloved land. Men have been betrayed by their own native lands and peoples or raped by foreign powers. They live their life without hope, prevented from participating in historical reality, knowing that they do not belong to it and that they can belong to no other native land. Their love is too deep to hide this from them. Without a foundation for their lives they hover in an empty space, bereft of history, thrown back on themselves alone by a pitilessly indifferent world.

Yet, as with the forsaken lover, the transformation can follow that Plato was the first to consummate. For all time he showed how it is possible. Reasoning about the conditions and origins of the common life develops from the love which is born out of loss and from the despair of frustration. What does not yet exist in reality must be prepared in thought. This thinking will be shaped by the world-historical situation. If a man, looking at what may be coming, has to admit that he has been rejected by his political fatherland, then he will not be accepted by another native land that does not exist, but by the fatherland of human history. With his thinking he helps to prepare the coming of world citizenship. He looks for confirmation of his being at home in humanity as such. From the disaster that has overtaken his own historical origin, from what was noble in the past of his own native land, from the heritage of his great ancestors, always supported by the historical origins of his love, he now finds his way to the source of humanity, of concrete historical humanity. As a human being he will be related to all human beings as if they were all one great family. This is not a natural process but only becomes possible when a man is reborn through Reason.

It appears that in ruin, so long as life has not been destroyed, Reason is able to turn the authentic personal existence of a man into new possibilities of constructive living—and when that happens, the authentic personal existences of isolated men come upon each other, calling out to one another across the world.

[62]

Let me end by repeating what Reason could be.

Where Reason provides a space, illusions disappear, frenzy and ferocity pass away. Life becomes existence, devoted to a purpose related to Transcendence.

The existence of Reason makes life a venture, but not an adventure, makes it prodigal but not wasteful. In the space provided by Reason existence can turn all temporal things into filled historicity, as unique concretions of the eternal.

Then Reason illuminates the relation between the historical and the supra-historical, seeks for the origin at the place to which no one can really attain in the consciousness of finite, temporal life.

The man who has once tasted Reason can never let it go again.

Many years ago I spoke about existentialism and at the time I added that it was not a new or special philosophy of its own but the one eternal philosophy. Since this had been momentarily lost in the merely Objective I argued that it was permissible to characterise it by Kierkegaard's basic concept.

Today I should prefer to call Philosophy the philosophy of Reason, since it appears urgently necessary to stress this age-old essence of philosophy. Once Reason is lost, philosophy itself is lost. From

[63]

the very beginning its task has been and still remains to acquire Reason, to restore itself as Reason which, whilst submitting to the necessities of the intellect and making the intellect entirely its own, does not succumb to its restrictions.

Reason appears as the outline of man's life, as we hope he will be and in so far as it lies within our power to create him. It is a life that is open to all men, which brings them into relationship and at the same time not only permits but demands the historical fulfilment of every single irreplaceable human life. Reason as a fundamental attitude would be the connecting link between persons alien to one another, of different historical origin. It would make possible a growing communication between the developing manifoldness which knows itself held together within the Unity which belongs to no one and to which all belong.

But, perhaps I hear one of you saying: 'To talk about Reason is like talking about a dream; all the things you have spoken of today are things that do not exist.'

I agree, they do not exist as the objects of an ascertaining intelligence but only as the content of a decision.

This decision can give reality to such facts as are

in their origins inaccessible to all causal knowledge. I can know causally solely that which is without Reason; it is only with Reason itself that I can understand the 'reasonable' which I meet in all the great things of history and in those facts which are not merely historical but which live on as an eternal present.

If I say that all this is a figment of the imagination it means that I do not want it to be a reality. Reason does not depend, however, on my knowledge of it but on my putting it into practice, in the sciences, in everyday life and in intellectual works that penetrate more deeply into the truth than the sciences are able to do.

Reason dares to rely upon itself in a world of Un-Reason and in face of its constant perversion into Anti-Reason.

III

REASON IN ITS STRUGGLE

REASON appears to have no enemy in so far as it tries to give light and speech to everything that exists, drawing it into relation with itself. It stretches out its hand in all directions, making no exceptions.

But in fact it meets resistance and an enemy that is out to destroy. In opposing this enemy, philosophy is transformed into the self-assertion of Reason, forced to suspend not its devoted effort to understand the enemies of Reason but its readiness to acknowledge them. Philosophy, which is the power of communication in the loving struggle of critical progress, is forced, when it faces its sole enemy, to become polemical, intellectually polemical, hurling questions and assertions into the battle.

This enemy is the unphilosophical spirit which knows nothing and wants to know nothing of truth. Under the name of truth it gives currency to everything that is inimical and alien to truth, to all the perversions of truth.

[66]

Wherever it reigns its violence makes careful study and enquiry impossible. It permits arbitrary actions and destroys self-control. It favours the violent passions of the moment, and extinguishes seriousness. It forces life from unbelief into fanatical pseudo-belief and then back again into nothingness.

This spirit is as changing and inconstant as Proteus, who did not let himself be grasped.

Refutation seems to give it new life, like the Lernean snake on which for every head destroyed two new ones grew.

We meet this enemy in the outside world, but, more dangerously, it lurks inside each one of us. We have already succumbed to it if we imagine we have overcome it.

Whence does this enemy derive its power? There is something inside all of us that yearns not for reason but for mystery—not for penetrating clear thought but for the whisperings of the irrational—not for the prudence of unprejudiced sight and hearing but for the capricious surrender to the darkness of multifariousness—not for the insights of humility but for gnostic omniscience to the point of absurdity—not for science but for wizardry disguised as science—not for rationally founded influence,

[67]

but for magic—not for loyalty, but adventure—not for the freedom which is one with reason and law and with the choice of one's own historicity, but for blind unrestraint and at the same time for blind obedience to a force that tolerates no questions.

What is the cause of this yearning for mystery, irrationality, absurdity, wizardry, magic, adventure, and finally for blind unrestraint and blind obedience at one and the same time?

When Reason is no longer supported and permeated by the whole personality of a man, when it slides back into mere intellect, this world of intellect gives rise to an intolerable sense of dissatisfaction. Reason, no longer understood, seems to be empty, mere nothing, a world of pale abstractions and meaningless, endlessly multiplying forms.

The very substance of our being yearns for fulfilment, for satisfaction and incarnation in the present. But the access to such fulfilment can be of two kinds. It can lead to a genuine fullness under the guidance of reason and to a historically continuing development through reason. Or it can produce a merely deceptive realisation, lost in the dispersal and anarchy of random multifariousness, without reason and contrary to reason.

Here is the parting of the ways between reason

[68]

and unreason. It is here that the road to disaster begins, with the betrayal of the simple truths that the decent, honest man usually takes for granted in his daily life.

After the betrayal has occurred the only way out is in a radical conversion in which one sees through oneself and assumes the guilt. Again and again we all stand at these cross-roads, faced with the possibility of becoming ourselves through Reason.

This is the ever-repeated decision, the possibility of becoming oneself, of becoming free, which coincides with the way to truth, with the simple honesty and integrity of the man whose smallest gestures are the expression of his real self. Here are the origins of the strength in which the mind works on its problems and on itself. Here is the beginning of the building up of historical content in the sphere of Reason, in which nothing is forgotten.

But if the possibility of willing one's life on a basis of Reason is abandoned at these cross-roads, it reappears in a perverted guise. Then our nature, failing to find satisfaction in itself, is impelled, even whilst denying truth, passionately to move towards an alleged truth. Knowing itself to be lost, it tries to deceive itself about its betrayal by fastening on to something of overpowering significance, something

[69]

it does not really grasp, but which has an objective existence in the world, and to which it can surrender the possibility of self-being and receive it back as acknowledged self-will.

This urge to escape from oneself to the point of complete self-forgetfulness, leads to the world of hazy ideologies which offer themselves as authentic truth, to the unreasonable, to absurdities which claim to be profundities, to aesthetic licence and poetic anarchism, to hyper-intellectual constructions which mean nothing at all and to the dialectic (this expression of the flux of caprice) which enables every decision to be abandoned, everything to be contradicted and everything justified. It leads, in a word, to the witches' sabbath of metaphorical talk, dogma and absolutes, of an endless retracing of one's steps, ever-changing interpretations of life, for which interpretation is no longer the way to the source but a fathomless end in itself, the dead end of interpreting interpretations.

The shapes of anti-reason which arise from the betrayal of truth and selfhood are the perversion of an original truth. Anti-reason uses the language of reason; all non-philosophy uses that of philosophy.

Thus, myth is the indispensable language of

transcendent truth. The creation of the genuine mythus is true illumination. This myth contains reason within itself and submits to the control of reason. Through the myth, through images and symbols we gain our deepest insight on the boundary.

When the process is perverted, however, it is quite different. Then the propensity to myth, uncontrolled by reason, leads to an indulgence in images for their own sake. The purpose is no longer the permeation by reason of the essence that is present in the images which represent one side of reality in the practical life of everyday. The urge is rather to be disengaged from the reality for which one is personally responsible and, by yielding to the enticing spectre of the irrational, to transfer it to a mysterious reality outside oneself. All that remains is a wildly roaming imagination committed to nothing which claims to be the truth of being, an inconsequential emotionalism. Mythical thinking like this which has drifted away from Reason is non-thought, because it lacks the animating force of existential self-criticism.

From the very beginning of philosophical thought the philosophy of Reason has been confronted by

[71]

non-philosophy, not as a powerless nonentity but as a powerful magic.

There is often an element of wizardry in great minds. To be skilled in magic is at times a great gift. Some of the great phenomena of German Idealism belong to this sphere; for example, Fichte's description of his own age as a turning-point and of his own philosophy as the crucial achievement of this turning-point. And the same pattern recurs in Nietzsche. Nietzsche's prophetic vision wavers awkwardly between deep insight and fraudulent deception. Marx's eschatology has the same fundamental flaw. But what is an obsession, an objective subjectivism in these great men is merely disgusting in smaller minds: the tendency to declare one's own thinking absolute, the only true thinking, egocentrically to identify oneself with the object, and to reject whatever conflicts with one's own interests and ideas. Such minds look not for friends but for admirers and obedient followers. They assess everyone purely according to the potential contribution he can make to their own self-aggrandizement.

But one single person is never merely a magician and not one of us is impervious to the seductions of magic. When we contrast the figure of the philosopher with that of the magician, we must avoid assigning anyone wholly to one category or the other.

The philosopher knows what he is doing when he thinks and acts; the magician does not know what he is doing nor how he is doing it. Both of them hit and miss the truth, but the philosopher incessantly corrects the content of what he considers true and becomes the master of his ideas; the magician examines not so much the truth as his own gestures, modes of expression and ways of impressing others. The philosopher tests the truth by searching for counter-arguments and enemies. The magician refuses to have his truth put to the test; he seems to be blind to the difference between truth and untruth, reality and appearance. He cannot really converse with others; he cannot engage in a candid discussion. He is biassed by his ideas, both by those he forms for himself and those he takes over. He goes through life a personification of the will to power, never seeing through his own motives.

The enemy lurks in all of us. To fight it, we have to fight ourselves. No philosophy becomes true without a conscious detachment from magic, from every form of magic, however sublime, whether scientifically encysted or poetically alluring. Kant carried out this process of self-cleansing in his treatise on Ghost-Seers.

But the effectiveness of philosophical magic depends on the compliance of the bewitched. The magician can be swept off his feet by a responsive audience eager to give themselves in worship. His force will be intensified and his authority confirmed by a crowd of admirers ready to nominate him a turning-point in the world's history and eager to place themselves at his disposal, to serve him and be despised by him.

The masses have followed the magicians again and again. The fraud has been perpetrated by the promise of absolute knowledge, by the claim that the magician's thought and action are of trans-cendental importance. Again and again the trick has succeeded by means of a total view of things of which the magician makes himself the centre of attraction and the turning point. An aura of magical efficacy has been produced. The number of sophists, aesthetes, quacks, of the late classical swindlers mocked by Lucian and the 'scientific' magicians of today is legion. Socrates and Plato were the first to take up the struggle against them in clear awareness of what was at stake.

It certainly looks as if the magicians, though rivals amongst themselves, realise their mutual affinity and cultivate a fellow feeling for one another. In a tacit, instinctive confederacy they stand arrayed against the one deadly enemy they have in common: Reason.

The growing strength of anti-reason, as it develops in the give and take between wizards and bewitched, is furthered by those who have not yet made up their minds, who take the absurdities of the magicians seriously and grant them a certain validity under the cloak of scientific objectivity. Some try out the magic for themselves first, with the mental reservation that they will reject it if it proves a failure (this was the attitude many people took to Hitler). But this is really neither psychologically nor practically feasible. Those who venture on this path, instead of throwing the light of Reason into this darkness as soon as it appears in them, are already almost lost.

Empty and devoid of the dignity of authentic personality non-reason follows a Pied Piper of Hamelin who stages the deception only half-aware of what he is doing. His unphilosophical ideas seem harmless enough when they first make their strange noises in a free world. But they have political significance.

With the surrender of the freedom of Reason this negation of philosophy prepares men for political

[75]

slavery. With its tendency to the mythical it causes the knowledge of freedom to founder. It teaches men to withdraw into the sphere of an unquestionable faith without Reason. When a man's life is no longer based on freedom he soon ceases to know what freedom is. Because he feels empty, and has lost both himself and the truth, in his fear he wishes to be cast down. By renouncing Reason, he has, without noticing the fact, renounced freedom. He is ready for any kind of totalitarianism and follows the ringleader to destruction, crime and a shameful death along with the rest of the herd.

For many years now we have been told that the menace of Nazism and Communism can be met only by opposing another faith to the one they represent. The free world is weak, it is said, because it is not supported by a faith.

In philosophy, too, rational thought often seems to have lost heart. On this matter I should like to offer the following reflections:

1. It looks today as if Reason, this comprehensive power of communication, which can even bring about mutual understanding between natures inherently alien to one another, is, paradoxically enough, being pushed into an isolation where

communication is impossible. It is as though, without any pre-arranged plan, all the powers of the mind were instinctively allied, because they have only one thing in common, the urge to make Reason disappear and to put some grandiose absurdity in its place. Whoever denies the very possibility of communication finds Reason for doing so in his own experience and confirmation of what appears to be his heroic affirmation of the inevitable loneliness of all men.

2. The life of Reason acts like the air, as though it were not there at all. How else can it act? It is in fact the pure air that should be the greatest necessity of life but which is usually spurned in favour of a narcotising and intoxicating atmosphere. Philosophy that only creates the air in which it is possible to grow, to come to oneself, to test oneself, is also intangible like the air. It gives nothing, issues no commands, demands no obedience, has nothing tangible to offer that can simply be taken away. It demands one's own thinking and one's own development; it helps one to attain them but it does not give them ready-made. Philosophy mercilessly presupposes the possibility of freedom when man secretly yearns to be taken by the hand—when he really wants to live in the fraudulent freedom of

obedience. Philosophy requires us to breathe freely, but it presupposes the existence of men capable of breathing. Is it a false claim that men ought to be themselves and ought to be free, or is it simply the illusion of an age that has now had its day? Are we not moving into another and superior form of life in which no one is any longer himself but everyone is all and all everyone, in which individuality and personality belong to the lumber of the past and to its self-deceptions?

Those who accept that view either abuse the philosophy of Reason as old-fashioned, eighteenth century 'enlightenment', traditional and behind the times, or more politely dismiss it.

3. Historical observation seems to show that all the great religious movements have been rooted in an element of absurdity and that it was this that enabled them to achieve their great effects. Reason is confronted again and again with the fact of a mass of believers who have lost all ability to listen, who can absorb no argument and who hold unshakeably fast to the Absurd as an unassailable presupposition—and really do appear to believe. Such considerations incline Reason to lose not only its illusions but all hope as well.

Such despondency is the expression of the undogmatic faith of Reason dying into mere intellectualism. Consciousness of his emptiness, a man tries to make a faith for himself in the political realm. In vain.

Or on the other hand, this despondency may not be a real despondency at all. When the faith of freedom breathes too little for lack of air—for lack of response—then, though it still trusts in itself in the last resort, it no longer has any hope of its own realisation in the present world.

There is only one way to overcome this feeling of hopelessness. Anyone who seriously wants to escape from the fog of the irrational, knows from his own freedom the basic experience that is never a gift of nature; he has the certainty that is not supported by any objective guarantee—he goes his way conscious of serving the truth, without possessing it.

He tries to save Reason in a world of will o' the wisps, to let its imperturbable patience speak despite the impotence of an apparently dying echo.

The faith of Reason is different in character from all the other faiths which are determined by denominational creeds, objective certainties and guarantees. It cannot engage in propaganda, it cannot hypnotise, it has nothing tangible to offer.

Where it exists, it is flexible on the surface but stubborn and unbending in the depths.

To help Reason to hold its own several lines of thought can be tried, thoughts in favour of Reason which may have as encouraging an influence as those others can be discouraging.

Anyone who has once tasted Reason must inevitably ask himself: what is there for me to will, if I forgo Reason? Once I have let it go, I cannot will Unity, the One, nor a historical structure guided by the Origin and Goal. I can only drift, wanting something different every day, today this, tomorrow that; and within a forced finiteness it may be possible to be intellectually consistent, though my intellect has become a perversion of Reason.

As in every historical age there are clear-thinking, upright men in the world today. Some of them have trod the way of Reason from their earliest days, though secretly and in seclusion. For Reason makes no noise. When it hears the charges levelled against it—accusing it of being old-fashioned, traditionalistic and 'enlightened'—reproaches which are fundamentally really eulogies—then it realises that it is a historical phenomenon in its modes of expression though not in its essence. As Reason it is for ever timely because what is eternally true can come to light only through the medium of Reason; and today as always men are listening to discover whether Reason can give language to their experience.

Even when the worst prognosis of decline is made, Reason refuses to accept it. When all the probabilities of the historical situation have been taken into account, the average qualities of the myriad human race, and the slavery and self-oblivion that have marked such great stretches of the human story, Reason still considers the forecast of ultimate catastrophe uncertain. Practical experience of unexpectedly favourable outcomes of apparently hopeless situations makes a deep impression. They are no proof that the same thing will happen again but they are, as it were, a guide for Reason in its basic attitude, which is to endure the tension, not to reckon with a certain future, to be conscious of the constant threat of disaster even in the most favourable circumstances, but not to overlook the range of possibilities in what may appear to be the most hopeless situations, and above all to keep on hoping; in any case to live, taking all the intellectual precautions possible and to decide one's course of action as conscientiously as may be within the limits of the possible, in the activity of production—like the peasants on Mount Vesuvius who bring their glorious fruits to maturity under the constant threat of the all-engulfing lava.

I think we can apply this to the course of world history too. Faced with the depressing probabilities no knowledge can prove the probability of the opposite. But the possibility of Reason prevailing is open and Reason must always be ready and prepare for it. And in his own small way it is the duty of the individual to help to prepare for it too. At any moment the general change may come which is always first experienced by the individual. Then the damp fogs which seemed to stifle almost everything may lift and man's awakening selfhood will listen, respond to and unite with the selfhood in other men.

But all the reasons and possibilities which thought can devise are not crucial for Reason. Reason lives from its origin, not by argument or by rejecting counter-argument, conscious in every moment of never being in possession of the truth but of being on the way to it.

Reason lives in the awareness of standing before the gates. Only in the bright realm of freedom does it seem possible for the strength to grow which will perhaps enable those who have held their ground to march through the gates. It may be, though, that the way will lead first through the darkness of thoughtless slavery, bound by symbols and the worship of man. Faced with this extreme possibility, the individual's decision to become himself and therefore a trustworthy partner in alliance with his friends, may become stronger and more deliberate. He will see that it is his duty to play no part, however unconsciously, in helping to bring about a complete surrender to a life that has become an empty mechanism of power, movement and nationalism, in which he participates without truth and sincerity.

Even then Reason cannot know for certain, but it also cannot regard it as impossible, that the worst horrors may be experienced to make possible a fundamental change in man. Man would be exposed to the worst, to the extent of even losing his own self, so that one day Reason might enter human reality again with an all-transporting power.

The crucial point to remember is, however, that nothing that belongs to Reason comes about automatically. It comes only through the active self-realisation of Reason itself. To the extent that Reason is active in the world it allows the hope to grow that its self-assertion against the powers of anti-reason and un-reason will succeed.

We know that we are all at the mercy of events outside our control. But within this destiny to which

[83]

we are bound to submit, man wants to try, nevertheless, in his own power of decision, to live a life of Reason, to experience selfhood and meaning with the aid of Reason.

Reason can stand firm only in the strength of Reason itself. When it understands its own meaning it is one with a basic trust in the origin of things, in other men and in itself.

I have spoken of Reason in its struggle, of its self-assertion which originates in the fact that it knows its powerlessness, and of the hope that inspires it when it is actively at work. All this takes place in the individual.

Reason's struggle, in so far as it can be prepared by purely intellectual effort, has its place in the universities, where everything open to scientific research can become the object of enquiry. Here the life of learning achieves wholeness through the mutual intercourse and discussion of scholars and scientists. Here too philosophy and theology have their place in order to attain in a fruitful tension the maximum self-consciousness through Reason in the world of learning.

Such is the Western idea of the university. The fact that the reality often falls short of the ideal, approaches it only step by step or falls away from it altogether, is no argument against its truth. The Idea has always been working in secret or as a possibility. To condemn the universities outright, to declare them hopelessly degenerate and lost, seems to me contemptible, for it is a way of thought that leads to inevitable disaster.

But self-criticism is also part of the idea of the university. At all time students and teachers alike should be aware of its present situation, should know what it was like in the past and what it might become in the future.

The struggle for Reason takes place in every branch of learning, but most consciously of all in philosophy. We know that philosophy plays only a modest part in the university today. One indication of this is the small but significant fact that even in the so-called philosophical faculty (from which, in the positivist age, the mathematics and science faculty was stupidly separated) appointment committees are filled by representatives of the departments related to the position to be filled, but philosophy itself is not regarded as being related to any other department! We owe the fact that philosophy is still taught at all to a medieval tradition that happens to have been retained and is still tolerated. But no

[85]

weight is attached to it. It is simply a hobby for a few individuals. Since Marx, in fact, there has been talk of the 'end of philosophy'. In the modern University of Jerusalem which has developed out of the needs and conditions of our own time, even the name of a philosophical faculty has been dropped. There philosophy has a modest place in the Faculty of Humanities in a special group of 'General Humanities' which is subordinate to other groups.

How has this come about? The cause seems to me to be first the wholesale departmentalisation of current thinking in a mass of specialised disciplines and the collapse of the breadth of Reason into mere intellectualism. Furthermore, and most important of all, it is due to the lack of a philosophy which measures up to the dimensions of the Reason that does in fact exist in the modern world and the lack of philosophers equal to the task of working out such a philosophy.

It is easy enough to criticise academic philosophy. We grew up in the midst of this criticism ourselves and have since become one of its targets. We university philosophers are accused of being purely academic, ignorant of the world, merely scientific, occupied with matters of no consequence, smugly unconcerned about fundamental human issues.

[86]

Nietzsche broke into this closed world of academic philosophy and carried off with him many young men who were longing for real philosophy. They scoffed at the solemnity and professorial security of current academic philosophy. They put the stress on actual experience and life, but though this made its appeal, it was quickly realised that it was merely a half-measure, as for instance in the line deriving from Dilthey whose philosophy, though apparently serious, had yielded to a purely interpretative knowledge of all kinds of bygone philosophies. The artificial-seeming objectivity, an imitation of the mathematicians, the forced simplicity which was intended to emphasise authenticity, and for that very reason produced an impression of unauthenticity and self-consciousness—all this was seen through.

This neglect of genuine philosophy, which nevertheless produced a good deal of useful research, was matched by a reluctant public that also failed to find the right path. What most people wanted, and generally all too quickly, was something quite different from philosophy though still masquerading under its name. Personal problems which failed to reach the realm of pure reason found satisfaction in psychoanalysis, and Marxism provided the great illusion for those who, dissatisfied with the current

[87]

state of the world, had an urge to see great events and to participate in world history. Feeling forsaken in the realm of pure Reason they wanted a substitute for religion and found it in sectarian movements devoted to artificially created celebrities who, on various levels, allowed themselves to become the objects of a kind of worship. Instead of thinking philosophically, they all wanted a total knowledge about the fundamentals of things, which seemed guaranteed by the authority of their magicians.

With such developments in mind it certainly seems to follow that it is necessary to cancel philosophy from the list of pursuits to be taken seriously and at the most to let it carry on its superfluous game a little longer in an academic annexe. The questions: who is engaged in philosophy? to whom do they address themselves? find no clear answer, unless one says that the philosopher is man himself, the thinking rational being turning to other thinking men, awaiting answer and question, in order to advance to the truth in a common effort. But if the answer is going to be as vague as all that one might just as well say: 'Philosophy is speaking from one vacuum to another'.

It is the magnificently Indefinite from which a criterion for our concrete philosophising comes.

[88]

With our eyes fixed on the sublime Idea we are trying constantly to translate it into reality. But some continuing institution or other is absolutely necessary if any possibility of philosophical thought is to remain open at all. For the Western world it is the university that holds open the possibility of a return to Reason and of a renewal of its influence. It is a doubtful possibility but the only real chance that remains. The intellectual struggle for Reason is bound to call on the university, for it is the legitimate dwelling place of pure Reason.

The teaching of philosophy is based on and presupposes special study. It maintains the philosophical tradition; its task is to impart knowledge of the categories and methods of thought, which is not in itself philosophy but only the technique without which philosophy cannot attain clarity—its task is further to discover the simple essential truths embedded in the vast mass of what has been thought.

A philosophy that isolated itself would be without Reason. Philosophy as a special subject is a questionable affair. As a teaching subject its task is no more than to direct attention.

The study of philosophy, then, is accomplished through the study of the sciences and the activity of one's own life, inspired by the great *philosophia perennis*.

It is through Reason that the teacher of philosophy has his place in the struggle for Reason. Of this struggle, whose sole weapons are intellectual and in which all the weapons are handed over to the enemy, we may say: In order that complete impartiality shall arise in the world of thought thinking people must be inwardly independent. And inward independence is possible only when man's will to power has ceased to exist, and perhaps only when he is in a state of powerlessness. Powerlessness seems the condition for acting in real freedom and for arousing freedom in others. In selfless humility, bereft of selfwill, the individual has a chance to take a minimal part in helping to create an atmosphere in which truth can thrive.

The teaching of the universities, our own work, stands with the rest of the traditional world in the shadow of a great menace which has been constantly growing since 1914. Ever since then the question, swiftly forgotten in a few years of peace, has been: What remains essential in view of the possible speedy end of everything we love?—What are the criteria that still hold good when the end of everything is approaching?

It seems to us to be beneath human dignity to waver between a destructive fear—which inhibits all activity—and a self-forgetful and blinkered ease in which old habits of thought continue, in which the intellectual life is no longer directed by Eros but an aimless thoughtless busyness is its only content, and work is done solely for the sake of work, regardless of the cause it ultimately serves.

The task of Reason in the face of this menace is to endure the tension, to do what is essential, to submit its daily life to the illuminated criteria, indefatigably to continue an activity that is inevitably only possible on a long-term basis. No one knows whether it will lead to success, or whether failure is its true meaning and end. But in an apparently hopeless situation Reason will never lose all hope. All those who work in the world of the mind must say to themselves: So long as I remain alive in the midst of terrible events, I intend to be prepared, to the best of my ability. I am trying to build up a life of inner activity with a goal that was set by my good genius, that is not wholly clear but is clear in respect to the step that has to be taken today under the actual conditions of my life.

It is our duty to fill the present time with a content.

[91]

Time is not given us to neglect. Only in a fully lived present can there be a meaning for the future. Without our planning, the fact that we do what we can in the present makes the future possible.

But if the knowable realities of human life tempt us to doubt Reason, then taking our criterion from these realities, we may rather say: it is a miracle that philosophy continues its way through history, that it has never completely disappeared since it first came on the scene, that there is a power of self-preservation in Reason which is realised repeatedly as freedom. Reason is like an open secret that can become known to anyone at any time; it is the quiet space into which everyone can enter through his own thought.

Author's Note to page 22, (added for the English edition)

What I have to say on pp. 22 ff. about psychoanalysis as a faith has led some readers to overlook my rather brief expression of appreciation—which is today a matter of course—of the individual insights of certain investigators who speak in the name of psychoanalysis, especially Freud himself. The boundary between knowledge which can be tested and unprovable assertions, and especially between knowledge and a view held in the name of faith is, it seems to me, not clearly drawn in the wider circle of psychoanalysts today. In this lecture I am concerned not with the knowledge but with this fateful trend of psychoanalytical faith. Part of that knowledge is, for example, the observation of transpositions in cases of hysteria (in the work of Breuer and Freud), and of the extraordinary significance of experiences in infancy and early childhood; the effect of certain experiences in many physical illnesses such as asthma, ulcers of the stomach, Graves's disease, and so on; the attention which has been drawn to the effect of certain violent suppressions of memory, to the connexions of meaning which can be seen in cases of psychosis and to the healing effect of confession. The reference to the soul in contrast to the earlier isolated observation of physical phenomena is, in general, a great gain. Just as Marx had many concrete insights and fruitful questions which arose independently of his thought as a faith (which finally triumphed over the rest), and just as the theorists about race pointed to a field of study and did discover some things, whereas their total view of man became an eccentric faith, in the same way many important discoveries have been made in the sphere of psychoanalysis. I have attempted to discuss these matters both critically and positively in theoretical psychology and in practice, in my *Allgemeine Psychopathologie*, 5th edition 1948, especially pp. 251–374, 563–598, and 661–686. In my book *Man in the Modern Age* (1931), I drew parallels between Marxism, psychoanalysis and the theory of race, as veiling in very different ways our true picture of man, and at the same time I pressed for a methodical development of genuine particular knowledge in these spheres. Further scientific development, which in respect of psychoanalytical facts and questions is still fluid, will show what is to endure scientifically as necessary knowledge.

A BIBLIOGRAPHY OF
KARL JASPERS' WRITINGS

Allgemeine Psychopathologie. 1913. Fifth edition 1948.
748 pages. Springer-Verlag, Heidelberg and
Berlin.

Psychologie der Weltanschauungen. 1919. Third edition
1925. 486 pages. Springer-Verlag, Heidelberg
and Berlin.

Strindberg und van Gogh. 1922. Third edition will
shortly be published by Joh. Storm-Verlag,
Bremen. 131 pages.

Max Weber, Rede bei der Trauerfeier. 1920. 30 pages.
Second edition 1926. Verlag Siebeck, Tübingen.

Die geistige Situation der Zeit. 1931. 191 pages. Seventh
edition will shortly be published by W. de
Gruyter & Co., Berlin. English edition: *Man
in the Modern Age* 1932, Routledge & Kegan
Paul.

Max Weber, Politiker, Forscher, Philosoph. 1932.
Second edition 1946. 58 pages. Joh. Storm-
Verlag, Bremen.

[94]

Philosophie. Three volumes. 1932. Second edition, one volume 1948. 913 pages. Springer-Verlag, Heidelberg and Berlin.

Vernunft und Existenz. 1935. New edition 1947. 124 pages. Joh. Storm-Verlag, Bremen.

Nietzsche, Einführung in das Verständnis seines Philosophierens. 1936. Second edition 1947. 487 pages. Third edition will shortly be published by W. de Gruyter & Co., Berlin.

Descartes und die Philosophie. 1937. Second edition 1948. 104 pages. W. de Gruyter & Co., Berlin.

Nietzsche und das Christentum. 1946. 85 pages. Verlag der Bücherstube Fritz Seifert, Hameln.

Die Idee der Universität. 1946. 132 pages. Springer-Verlag, Heidelberg and Berlin.

Vom lebendigen Geist der Universität. 1946. 40 pages. Verlag Lambert Schneider, Heidelberg.

Die Schuldfrage. 1946. 106 pages. Verlag Lambert Schneider, Heidelberg, and Artemis-Verlag, Zürich, 96 pages.

Antwort an Sigrid Undset u. a. Aufsätze. 1947. 31 pages. Südverlag, Konstanz.

Vom europäischen Geist. 1947. 31 pages. R. Piper & Co. Verlag, München. English edition, *The European Spirit.* S. C. M. Press 1948. 64 pages.

Der philosophische Glaube. 1947. 136 pages. Second edition 1948. R. Piper & Co. Verlag, München, and Artemis-Verlag, Zürich, 158 pages. English edition, *The Perennial Scope of Philosophy*, 1951. Routledge & Kegan Paul.

Von der Wahrheit. 1947. XXIV, 1103 pages. R. Piper & Co. Verlag, München.

Unsere Zukunft und Goethe. 1948. 43 pages. Artemis-Verlag, Zürich, and Joh. Storm-Verlag, Bremen.

Philosophie und Wissenschaft. 1949. 16 pages. Artemis-Verlag, Zürich.

Einführung in die Philosophie. Twelve Broadcast Talks, 1949. Artemis-Verlag, Zürich. English edition *The Way to Wisdom*, 1951. Victor Gollancz.

Vom Ursprung und Ziel der Geschichte. 1949. Second edition 1950. 349 pages. R. Piper & Co. Verlag, München.

Rechenschaft und Ausblick. 1951. R. Piper & Co. Verlag, München.